Paleo Seafood

Gluten Free, Wheat Free, Sugar Free, Flat Belly, Weight Loss Recipes

Contents

About the Book 4

Introduction 5

Breakfast 6

Smoked Salmon Breakfast Hash 6

Simple Shrimp Scampi Breakfast 7

Tilapia Fillet with Nuked Veggies 8

Spicy Salmon Cucumber Bites 9

Fiery Sautéed Mushrooms with Anchovy 10

Grilled Herb Stuffed Sardines 11

Shrimp & Avocado Omelet 12

Lunch 13

Salmon and Spinach Salad with Arugula Pesto 13

Shrimp stuffed Avocados 15

Honey Lime Glazed Salmon 16

Seafood Stew 17

Salmon Blueberry Lettuce Wraps 18

Spicy Tuna Salad 19

Paleo Marinated Grilled Swordfish 20

Tilapia Tacos 21

Paleo Garlic Shrimp Kabobs 22

Simple Herb Crusted Salmon 23

Dinner 24

Lemon-Tarragon Salmon 24

Shrimp, Tilapia & Cabbage Curry 25

Seafood & Leek Soup 26

Shrimp and Avocado Salad 27

Paleo Halibut Ceviche 28

Lemon Garlic Tilapia 29

Tropical Tuna Ceviche 30

Shrimp, Cantaloupe and Mint Salad 31

Louisiana Fillets 33
Prawn & Chorizo Faux Spanish Rice 34
Desserts and Snacks 36
Pineapple Coconut Ice Cream 36
Carrot Cake 37
Sautéed Shrimp 38
Shrimp Cocktail 39
Bananas with Almond Butter and Coconut 40

About the Book

This book is for Paleo diet followers who love to eat delicious foods from the sea. Get more familiar with the Paleolithic diet and its health benefits in the introduction. Then in this book you will find a collection of recipes for every meal of the day. Start your day with a healthy start eating a delicious breakfast made from salmon, tilapia fillet, sardines and lots more. Following breakfast, are lunch recipes that are light and delicious. Then comes the most important meal of the day dinner. The fiery dinner ingredients include seafood salad, soup, salsa and prawns. Lastly, indulge your sweet tooth without even breaking the rules! Enjoy the collection of delicious and nutritious recipes while following the Paleo guidelines.

Introduction

The Paleolithic diet is a way of eating from 10,000 years ago in the Paleolithic era, also known as the caveman diet, Stone Age diet and hunter gathered diet. The Paleo diet consists of foods that were eaten before the agricultural revolution and wheat based diet. This diet consists of meat, seafood, fruits, vegetables and nuts. All foods in their natural form, not processed and wheat free are included. Studies are showing that human bodies are better adapted to this way of eating.

Foods in their natural form contain a great deal of vitamins and minerals. By including these in daily eating, many health benefits may be achieved. Following the Paleo diet, people have reclaimed a healthy body weight, lowered cholesterol, decreased high blood pressure, decreased cardiac problems, experienced increased energy and stabilized blood sugar levels.

Paleo diets including seafood as main ingredient also have several health benefits. Seafood is low in saturated fats and high in omega-3 fatty acids. These fats protect the heart from disease and lower the amount of cholesterol in the blood. Researchers have highlighted and recommended that an extra share of seafood / fish in the diet each week can reduce the risk of heart disease by half. Regular use of seafood in the diet has shown to lessen the risk of various diseases and disorders like asthma, cancer, dementia, depression, diabetes and much more. Many of the traditional recipes that people love, have a Paleo version that are just as delicious, if not more so. An added bonus is you are giving your body the nutrients it needs, so there is no guilt. Best of luck on your journey eating clean with Paleo! These recipes can be a starting point to help you create new favorite meals.

Breakfast

Smoked Salmon Breakfast Hash

1 Serving

1/2 tbsp. butter

4 oz. wild salmon fillet (shredded) smoked

1/4 head of cabbage (chopped)

2 eggs (whisk)

3 tbsp. chicken broth

2 tbsp. coconut milk

Sea salt (to taste)

Pepper (to taste)

Take a medium skillet and melt the butter over medium heat. Combine the in the cabbage, broth, salt and pepper and sauté for few minutes until the cabbage is softened. Next whisk in the eggs, salmon, coconut milk, salt and pepper to taste. Mix together well and cook over medium-low heat until the eggs are cooked through. Serve hot.

Simple Shrimp Scampi Breakfast

1 Serving

1 lb. shrimp (melted & peeled)

1 lemon (squeezed)

1/4 cup of cooking sherry

1/2 cup fresh cilantro (chopped)

1 garlic clove (minced)

Combine and mix all the ingredients together in a frying pan. Stir it over medium-high heat for 5 to 7 minutes. Serve it with rice or mix in with broccoli.

Tilapia Fillet with Nuked Veggies

2-3 Servings

1lb. frozen tilapia filet

2 tbsp. butter

Ground pepper (to taste)

Chili finishing salt (to taste)

Frozen veggies (optional)

Take a microwave safe dish and place the frozen tilapia filet and butter in it. Sprinkle it with some ground pepper and chili finishing salt. Wrap the dish to cover and nuke for 4-5 minutes and then let stand for 2 minutes. Combine different veggies (optional) and nuke until softened. Then serve tilapia filet with veggies.

Spicy Salmon Cucumber Bites

6-8 Servings

1/2 lb. salmon (cooked)

1 tbsp. shallots (minced)

1/4 c. Paleo mayonnaise

1/4 tsp. paprika (smoked)

1/4 tsp. Tabasco

1 tbsp. chives (chopped)

Kosher salt (to taste)

Freshly ground pepper (to taste)

1 cucumber (peeled & cut into 3/4" thick slices)

4 tomatoes (quartered)

1 bunch chive sprigs (for garnish)

Take a small bowl; add and mix mayonnaise, paprika and Tabasco thoroughly. Take the cooked salmon and crush it into large bite sized pieces. Put the salmon, shallots, salt, chives, and pepper in a bowl and gently mix in the spicy mayonnaise, taste and adjust the seasonings. Take a teaspoon and scoop out the center of each cucumber slice, like a cup. Add the salmon mixture into each cucumber cup and top each with tomato slice and a couple of chives.

Fiery Sautéed Mushrooms with Anchovy

2 Servings

2 medium anchovy fillets

2 tbsp. butter

1/4 tsp. hot red pepper chips

3 medium garlic cloves (minced)

1 lb. white mushrooms (halved)

Take a large skillet and melt the butter over medium-high heat. Add pepper flakes, garlic, and anchovy fillets and cook for 2 minutes or until the mixture is fragrant. Mix in the mushrooms, keep frying and stirring occasionally until the mushrooms are lightly browned. This takes about 12 minutes. Salt to taste and serve immediately.

Grilled Herb Stuffed Sardines

3 Servings

2 lb. fresh sardines

3 tbsp. butter

1/2 cup parsley (packed)

4 stalks green onions (chopped)

2 tbsp. bacon grease (melted)

1 large lemon

Kosher salt (to taste)

Pepper (to taste)

Pre-heat the oven to broil. Take a kitchen knife, cut a thin line along the belly of the fish and pull out the insides. Rinse and pat to dry, set aside. Take a food processor, mix in butter, parsley, green onions, salt, and pepper and pulse until a uniform paste is formed. Take 1 tablespoon of paste and fill each sardine cavity. Coat the sardine skin with bacon grease and sprinkle some salt and pepper. Put the sardines in oven on a wire rack/tray and broil for 5 minutes. Sliced up a lemon and served with the broiled sardines.

Shrimp & Avocado Omelet

2 Servings

4 eggs (beaten)

1/4 lb. shrimp (peeled & deveined)

1 medium tomato (diced)

1/2 avocado (diced)

1 tbsp. fresh cilantro (chopped)

1 tsp. coconut oil

Sea salt (to taste)

Freshly ground black pepper (to taste)

Take a frying pan add and cook the shrimp over medium heat until no pink remains, slice and set aside. Take a small bowl and mix the tomato, avocado and cilantro together. Flavor it with sea salt and freshly ground black pepper, set aside. Take a non-stick skillet; melt the coconut oil over medium-high heat. Pour half of the beaten eggs into the skillet; tip the pan gently to cover the skillet base with the eggs. When eggs are nearly fully stiffened, add shrimp pieces on top of one half of the egg. Fold the omelet in half and cook 1 to 2 minutes more. Add tomato & avocado mixture on top. Repeat the same process for second omelet.

Lunch

Salmon and Spinach Salad with Arugula Pesto

2-4 Servings

For Salmon

2 salmon filets

2 tbsp. arugula pesto

Salt (to taste)

Pepper (to taste)

For Arugula Pesto

2 c. fresh arugula

1 clove garlic

1/4 c. walnuts

1/2 c. olive oil

Salt (to taste)

Pepper (to taste)

For Salad

3 cup spinach

2 cup micro greens

1 cup cabbage (shredded)

1 carrot (shredded)

1 cup green beans (cooked & chopped)

Add salt and pepper to both sides of the salmon filets, lay them on a baking sheet. Spread 1 tablespoon of arugula pesto on the top of the salmon filets. Bake the fish in a broiler for 5 minutes or until fish is flaking and opaque, set aside. For pesto, take a food processor, add and blend arugula, garlic and walnuts. Next mix in the olive oil and pulse to blend well. Transfer the pesto to a bowl and stir in salt and pepper to taste, cover and refrigerate. For making the salad, mix all the ingredients in a bowl. Put in 4 tablespoon of pesto and flip greens until well combined, set aside. Salmon and Spinach Salad with Arugula Pesto is now ready to serve.

Shrimp stuffed Avocados

4 Servings

4 large avocados (peeled & halved)

1/2 cup small salad shrimp (cooked & washed)

1 tbsp. lemon juice

1 tbsp. onion powder

1 tsp. black pepper

1 tbsp. paprika

Salt (to taste)

Place the halved avocados on a serving plate with cut side facing up. Take a medium sized bowl, combine shrimp, lemon juice, onion, pepper and salt. Spoon the avocado with shrimp mixture into the avocado cup. Shake paprika on the top of each stuffed avocado before serving.

Honey Lime Glazed Salmon

2 Servings

2 fresh salmon fillets

2 tbsp. raw honey

2 tbsp. butter (melted)

2 tbsp. fresh lime juice

Sea salt (to taste)

Pepper (to taste)

Pre-heat the oven to 400 degrees. Line 9 × 9 inch pan with foil or parchment paper. Take a small bowl, beat butter, honey, lime juice, sea salt and pepper together. Put the fish fillets in the pan; sprinkle some sea salt and pepper on them. Place the glaze over the fillets, cover completely. Bake it for 15 to 20 minutes or until the fish is cooked through.

Seafood Stew

3 Servings

8 oz. raw shrimp (peeled & deveined)

4 oz. tilapia (cubed)

4 oz. crab meat

1 tbsp. vegetable oil

1 onion (chopped)

2 cloves garlic (minced)

14 oz. diced tomatoes (with juice)

1 ½ c. chicken broth

1/2 c. clam juice

Parsley & Basil (to taste)

Take a large frying pan and heat oil. Add onion and garlic and sauté until softened, season with parsley. Add in diced tomatoes, broth and clam juice. Add basil, salt and pepper (if needed). Cover up and simmer for about 30 minutes. Next add in the tilapia cubes, shrimp and crab meat and bring to a boil. Then lower heat, cover and simmer again for another 5 to 7 minutes.

Salmon Blueberry Lettuce Wraps

1-2 Servings

6 oz. salmon (boneless & skinless)

1/3 c. blueberries

1 tbsp. almonds (Slivered)

1/2 tbsp. Chives (chopped)

4 leaves Romaine or baby lettuce

Paleo mayonnaise (as required)

Drain the salmon and place it in a medium sized bowl. Mix in mayonnaise, almonds, blueberries and chives. Mix to combine well. Lay the lettuce leaves in a plate and scoop the mixture into them.

Spicy Tuna Salad

2 Servings

2 cans tuna

1 c. green or black olives (chopped)

2 green onions (chopped)

1 jalapeno pepper (finely chopped)

3 tbsp. capers (rinsed)

1/2 tsp. red chili flakes

2 lemons (squeezed)

Olive oil for spray

1 head butter lettuce (optional)

1 avocado (sliced)

Take a large bowl, combine and mix all the ingredients together. Serve them over lettuce and top with sliced avocado. Serve instantly or store it in the refrigerator.

Paleo Marinated Grilled Swordfish

4 Servings

4 swordfish steaks

1 lemon (sliced into wedges)

1 tbsp. fresh parsley (optional)

For Marinade

1/3 c. chicken broth

3 cloves garlic (crushed)

1/4 c. fresh lemon juice

3 tbsp. olive oil

1/2 tsp. sea salt

1/2 tsp. ground black pepper

1/2 tsp. ground sage

1/2 tsp. rosemary

1/2 tsp. marjoram

Take a large plastic bad with a lid, add and combine all marinade ingredients together. Seal the bag and shake the marinade around to blend. Place the swordfish steaks into the marinade and place the sealed bag in the refrigerator. Preserve it for 1 to 3 hours; keep rotating the bag to make sure that the steaks are well coated. Take the steaks out of the bag and lay them on a plate. Grill for 5 to 6 minutes on each side. Shake parsley on top and serve with lemon wedges.

Tilapia Tacos

4 Servings

1lb fresh tilapia fillets

4 cloves garlic (minced)

2 jalapeño peppers (finely chopped)

2 c. tomatoes (diced)

1 tbsp. Paleo cooking fat

1 medium onion (chopped)

1/4 c. fresh cilantro (finely chopped)

3 tbsp. lime juice

Sea salt (to taste)

Freshly cracked black pepper (to taste)

1 avocado (sliced)

Take a large skillet and heat over a medium-high heat. Combine the cooking fat, garlic and onions, cook for about 5 minutes or until the onions becomes soft. Add the tilapia fillets into the skillet; allow the fillets to cook for 3 to 4 minutes on each side. When the fish begins to cook through, use a fork to smash it apart into flaky pieces. Mix in the jalapeno pepper, tomatoes, cilantro and lime juice. Season it with salt and pepper to taste. Bake 5 minutes more before turning off the heat. Garnish the taco filling with fresh avocado slices and serve.

Paleo Garlic Shrimp Kabobs

4 Servings

1/4 cup coconut oil

1 tbsp. sesame seeds

1 lb. shrimp (peeled & rinse)

4 cloves garlic (minced)

1 tbsp. lime juice

Take a medium bowl, combine and mix coconut oil, lime juice and garlic. Stir the shrimp into the bowl mixture. Seal the bowl & place in refrigerator for 4 to 5 hours. When it is ready then set the grill to medium heat. Skewer 6 shrimp per stick; baste skewers on each side with the marinade. Grill for few minutes on each side, until no longer pink.

Simple Herb Crusted Salmon

2 Servings

For the salmon

2 salmon fillets (12 oz)

1 tbsp. coconut flour

2 tbsp. fresh parsley

1 tbsp. olive oil

1 tbsp. Dijon mustard

Salt and pepper (to taste)

For the salad

2 cup arugula

1/4 red onion (thinly sliced)

1 tbsp. lemon juice

1 tbsp. white wine vinegar

1 tbsp. olive oil

Salt and pepper (to taste)

Pre-heat the oven to 450 degrees. Place salmon fillets on a parchment or foil lined baking sheet. Top the salmon with olive oil and Dijon mustard, spread over salmon. Take a small bowl, mix the coconut flour, parsley, salt and pepper together. Sprinkle it over the salmon and cover them well. Bake in the oven for 10 to 15 minutes or until salmon is cooked. Take a bowl, mix salad ingredients together. When salmon is ready, place salmon on top of salad and serve.

Dinner

Lemon-Tarragon Salmon

4 Servings

8oz salmon fillets (qty-04)

2 tbsp. fresh tarragon (finely chopped)

2tbsp. coconut oil or cooking oil

2 tsp. lemon zest

2 lemons

1/8 tsp. salt (to taste)

1/4 tsp. ground pepper (to taste)

Pre-heat the oven to 375 degrees. Take a small bowl and combine the tarragon, lemon zest, salt and pepper. Sprinkle it over the top of salmon fillets and place them on the baking sheet. Bake the fillets in the oven for 15 minutes or until opaque throughout. Squeeze lemon over the top and Serve.

Shrimp, Tilapia & Cabbage Curry

3-4 Servings

1 lb. raw shrimp

8 oz. tilapia fillets (qty-02)

6 c. cabbage (shredded into 1/4" strips)

2 medium carrots (shredded)

4 c. fresh spinach

1/3 c. chicken broth

2 tbsp. coconut oil

1 ½ tsp. Ginger (shredded)

1 tbsp. Curry Powder

1/2 tsp. salt (to taste)

1/4 c. coconut cream extract

First cut the tilapia fillets into ½ x 2 inch strips. Take a large frying pan and warm it over medium-high heat, add oil, broth, cabbage and carrot. Sauté and simmer the cabbage & carrots for 5 to 6 minutes or until soft. Move the cabbage & carrots to the outer edges of the pan and put all the seafood to the middle. Shake over the ginger, salt and curry powder in the pan and stir gently until evenly coated. Continue cooking for about 5-6 minutes until the seafood is completely cooked. Put spinach in and stir until wilted, then add coconut cream concentrate and stir to combine. Serve it warm.

Seafood & Leek Soup

6 Servings

4 c. fish stock or chicken bone broth

1 lb. mixed seafood (e.g. shrimp, calms, scallops, crabs, calamari, and lobster etc.)

6 oz. salmon (cut into large pieces)

6 oz. tilapia (cut into large pieces)

4 c. leeks (chopped)

1 c. dry white wine

2 tbsp. fresh parsley (chopped)

1 tsp. salt (to taste)

In a skillet, simmer the broth over high heat. Lower the heat and add seafood, fish & leeks to the broth. Sauté for 15 to 20 minutes until the seafood is fully cooked and leeks are softened.

Mix in parsley, wine & salt and again sauté for 5 to 6 minutes. Seafood & leek soup is now ready to serve.

Shrimp and Avocado Salad

2 Servings

For Salad

1 lb. shrimp (cooked, deveined & tail removed)

2 ripe avocados

4 c. lettuce

Cilantro dressing

For Cilantro Dressing/Marinade

3 tbsp. fresh lime juice

2 tbsp. olive oil

1/2 c. fresh cilantro (chopped)

1/8 tsp. fresh ground pepper (to taste)

Salt (to taste)

In a bowl, combine all the cilantro marinade ingredients and mix well. Pour this mixture over shrimp and stir to coat. Cover up and refrigerate it for 2 to 3 hours. Rinse and dry lettuce and divide among plates. Slice avocado into small bite size pieces and add over lettuce. Top with marinated shrimp and available dressing.

Halibut Ceviche

2 Servings

1lb halibut fillet (skinless, diced into 1/2" pieces)

1 lime (juiced)

1/4 c. fresh squeezed orange juice

1 pepper (habanera seeded & minced)

1 orange (peel and divide into sections)

Salt and pepper (to taste)

In a bowl and combine the in the fillet, juices, and pepper pieces. Wrap and refrigerate for about 3 hours. Strain liquid and toss with orange sections. Add in pepper and salt (to taste) and serve.

Lemon Garlic Tilapia

2 Servings

4 tilapia fillets

1 tbsp. olive oil

1 tbsp. butter or margarine

1tbsp. lemon juice

1 tsp. garlic salt

1 tsp. parsley flakes (dried)

Salt (to taste)

Cayenne pepper (to taste)

Pre-heat the oven up to 400 degrees. Coat the baking dish with olive oil. Add butter, olive oil, lemon juice, garlic powder, salt, parsley and sauté for a few minutes. Transfer it over tilapia fillets into the baking pan with some cayenne pepper on top. Bake in pre-heated oven for about 13 minutes and broil for an additional 2 to 3 minutes.

Tropical Tuna Ceviche

2-3 Servings

450 g. sashimi quality tuna (diced)

3 tbsp. lime juice

1 small orange (juice & zest)

1 bird's eye chili (chopped)

2 tsp. ginger (peeled & minced)

1/4 c. coconut milk

1/4 tsp. salt

Black pepper (to taste)

2 c. watercress (stems removed)

1/2 mango (peeled & diced)

Fresh coconut (thinly shaved)

Keep tuna in a mixture of the citrus juices & zest for about 60 minutes or until tuna is rare. Combine bird's eye chili, coconut milk, ginger, salt and pepper, toss in tuna. Mix in mango and watercress and toss to combine. Transfer it to serving bowls, garnish with coconut shavings and serve.

Shrimp, Cantaloupe and Mint Salad

4 servings

3 c. fresh Arugula

1/2 medium shrimp (pre-cooked)

1 c. fresh mango (cubed)

1 c. fresh cantaloupe (cubed)

3 tbsp. fresh lime or lemon juice

1 tsp. cinnamon

1 tsp. nutmeg

Take a bowl, mix the precooked shrimp, cubed mango, cubed cantaloupe, cinnamon, nutmeg and lemon or lime juice. Top the Arugula with the mixture and enjoy.

White Fish with Macadamia Salsa

2 Servings

2 fish fillets (white)

1/4 c. macadamia nuts (chopped)

1/2 c. tomatoes (diced)

1 avocado (peeled, seeded & diced)

3 tbsp. coriander (chopped)

3 tbsp. parsley (chopped)

Olive oil

Pre-heat the grill to medium heat. Place the fillets on the grill and cook for 3 to 4 minutes or until cooked through. To make the salsa, take a mixing bowl; combine the remaining ingredients together and mix well. Now the fish and macadamia salsa is ready. Place cooked fish and salsa onto serving plates and serve.

Louisiana Fillets

2 Servings

2 tbsp. coconut oil

1 lemon (squeezed)

2 firm white fish fillets (sole, snapper, trout, or catfish)

1/2 tsp. lemon pepper

1/8 tsp. red pepper (crushed)

1/8 tsp. garlic powder

Sea salt (optional)

Freshly ground black pepper (optional)

Pre-heat the oven up to 350 degrees. Take a medium oven proof skillet, melt the coconut oil with the lemon juice over medium high heat. Coat both sides of the fillets and place them side-by-side in the pan. Mix the spices up & sprinkle over the fillets. Cook in the oven for 20 to 25 or until ready. Season fillets with sea salt & freshly ground black pepper (optional).

Prawn & Chorizo Faux Spanish Rice

3-4 Servings

6 prawns (peeled and deveined)

1 medium chicken breast (diced)

1 medium chorizo (diced)

1/2 head of cauliflower (broken into florets)

1/2 brown onion (chopped)

1/2 red pepper (chopped)

1/2 long red chili (chopped)

3 garlic cloves (chopped)

1 tsp. sweet paprika

1 tsp. smoked paprika

1/4 tsp. saffron powder (optional)

1/2 lemon

1/4 c. white wine

1 tbsp. tomato paste

1/2 c. chicken or vegetable stock

Extra virgin olive oil

Sea salt (to taste)

Black pepper (to taste)

Take a large frying pan and warm 1 teaspoon of olive oil until hot. Add chorizo and cook on medium high heat for 1 to 2 minutes on both sides or until browned and crisp, set aside. Add prawns into the fats that are left from the sausage, cook on both sides for 1 minute. Sprinkle with a little salt and set it aside. At last add some more olive oil and the chicken, cook for about 2 minutes until slightly browned on all sides, set aside. Now add in garlic, a dash of salt and stir through until mixture starts to caramelize. Pour in white wine and let it bubble away for 30 seconds. Add tomato paste and stock, cook for 5 minutes over low heat until the onion and red peppers are softened and the sauce is slightly thickened. To finish, add the precooked chicken and faux cauliflower rice and mix through. Pour in more olive oil, a bit of salt, chorizo and prawns. Stir and cook it for about 2-3 minutes and sprinkle with some lemon juice to finish it off. Sprinkle with paprika and serve it with some green onions.

Desserts and Snacks

Pineapple Coconut Ice Cream

4 Servings

4 egg yolks

1 can full fat coconut milk

3 tbsp. raw honey

1 tbsp. vanilla extract

1/4 c. pineapple juice

3/4 c. fresh pineapple (finely chopped)

Take a medium sized sauce pan, add and combine the coconut milk, honey, vanilla extract, pineapple juice and bring to boil. In a small bowl beat the egg yolks until foamy, pour about ¼ of the hot coconut milk mixture into the egg yolks and whisk rapidly. Pour the combined mixture into the saucepan with the rest of the coconut milk mixture. Simmer and cook until thickened for about 5 minutes. Shift the custard into a bowl and refrigerate to cool. Now pour the chilled custard into an electric ice cream maker and add pineapple a few minutes prior to the end of the process. Keep it in freezer to chill until hard for 2 to 3 hours before serving.

Carrot Cake

9 Servings

6 eggs (divided)

1/2 c. raw honey (optional)

1/2 c. ripe carrots (pureed)

1 tbsp. orange zest

1 tbsp. orange juice (freshly squeezed)

3 c. almond flour

Coconut oil

Pre-heat the oven to 325 degrees. Take a medium bowl, whisk the egg yolks and honey simultaneously. Combine in carrots, orange zest, orange juice concentrate and almond flour. Take a small bowl and whisk the egg whites until stiff with a hand mixer, add it into a medium bowl. Stir into a batter. Lightly grease a 9' spring form pan and then transfer the batter into it. Bake in the oven for 50 minutes. Let cool in the pan for 15 minutes and then turn out onto a wire rack to cool completely.

Sautéed Shrimp

2 Servings

2 tbsp. coconut or olive oil

1/2 lb. raw shrimp (deveined and peeled)

2 tbsp. chili powder

1 tbsp. garlic powder

1/2 tbsp. parsley

Cayenne pepper (to taste)

Freshly ground black pepper (to taste)

Take a medium sized frying pan and melt the oil over medium-high heat. Add shrimp and cook for 1 minute. Mix in chili powder, parsley, garlic powder & cayenne pepper. Sauté for another 3 to 5 minutes or until shrimp is no longer pink and completely cooked.

Shrimp Cocktail

2 Servings

1 lb. shrimp (shelled & deveined)

2 tbsp. lemon juice

6 tbsp. chili sauce

1 tsp. onion (grated)

1/2 tbsp. horseradish

1 celery stalk (finely chopped)

2-4 lettuce leaves

Add water into frying pan and heat to boil. Place in the shrimp & turn off the heat. Allow shrimp to sit in the hot water for 3 to 5 minutes or until fully cooked. Take out cooked shrimp from water & rinse with cold water to chill instantly. Take a bowl and whisk chili sauce, horseradish, lemon juice and onion all together in order to make the cocktail sauce. Flip the shrimp with celery. Fill the cocktail cups with salad greens and spoon in the shrimp mixture. Top with sauce and serve chilled.

Bananas with Almond Butter and Coconut

2 Servings

1 large banana

2 tbsp. almond butter

2 tbsp. coconut milk

2 tsp. Slivered almonds, cinnamon or shredded coconut (as per taste)

Take two small bowls, slice the banana and divide it into bowls. Add almond butter & coconut milk in each bowl on top of each banana. Put in almonds, cinnamon or coconut for tasty variations.

Made in the USA
Middletown, DE
10 October 2014